FEARNON

The Origins and
Nature of the
Great Slump
1929-1932

9529048

338 54

HERTFORDSHIRE LIBRARY SERVICE

**Please return this book on or before the date shown below or ask for
it to be renewed.** Applications for renewal by post
or telephone should quote the date of return and the information on
the top of this label and, where applicable, the letter and number on
the date card. Books which have been previously renewed or which
are more than one week overdue can only be renewed by bringing
them to the library. Renewals cannot be granted on books in demand.

L.32A

9/12

17 DEC 2005

20 MAR 1982   -8 MAR 1994

17 FEB 1990   21 JAN 1997   20 MAR 2004

01 MAR 1994   30 JAN 2001   24 JAN 2006

                                         -2 MAR 2006
                              30 JAN 2008

2 0 OCT 2008

The Origins and Nature of the Great Slump 1929–1932

Prepared for
The Economic History Society by

PETER FEARON

Lecturer in Economic History,
University of Leicester

M

First published 1979 by
THE MACMILLAN PRESS LTD
London and Basingstoke
Associated companies in Delhi Dublin
Hong Kong Johannesburg Lagos Melbourne
New York Singapore and Tokyo

Printed in Great Britain

British Library Cataloguing in Publication Data

Fearon, Peter
  The origins and nature of the Great Slump, 1929–32.
  – (Studies in economic and social history).
  1. Depressions – 1929 – Europe
  2. Depressions – 1929 – United States
  I. Title   II. Series
  338.5′ 4′ 094   HB3782

  ISBN 0–333–19801–8

STUDIES IN ECONOMIC AND SOCIAL HISTORY

This series, specially commissioned by the Economic History Society, provides a guide to the current interpretations of the key themes of economic and social history in which advances have recently been made or in which there has been significant debate.

Originally entitled 'Studies in Economic History', in 1974 the series had its scope extended to include topics in social history, and the new series title, 'Studies in Economic and Social History', signalises this development.

The series gives readers access to the best work done, helps them to draw their own conclusions in major fields of study, and by means of the critical bibliography in each book guides them in the selection of further reading. The aim is to provide a springboard to further work rather than a set of pre-packaged conclusions or short-cuts.

ECONOMIC HISTORY SOCIETY

The Economic History Society, which numbers over 3000 members, publishes the *Economic History Review* four times a year (free to members) and holds an annual conference. Enquiries about membership should be addressed to the Assistant Secretary, Economic History Society, Peterhouse, Cambridge. Full-time students may join the Society at special rates.

STUDIES IN ECONOMIC AND SOCIAL HISTORY

Edited for the Economic History Society by T. C. Smout

PUBLISHED

OTHER TITLES ARE IN PREPARATION

Editor's Preface

SINCE 1968, when the Economic History Society and Macmillan published the first of the 'Studies in Economic and Social History', the series has established itself as a major teaching tool in universities, colleges and schools, and as a familiar landmark in serious bookshops throughout the country. A great deal of the credit for this must go to the wise leadership of its first editor, Professor M. W. Flinn, who retired at the end of 1977. The books tend to be bigger now than they were originally, and inevitably more expensive; but they have continued to provide information in modest compass at a reasonable price by the standards of modern academic publication.

There is no intention of departing from the principles of the first decade. Each book aims to survey findings and discussion in an important field of economic or social history that has been the subject of recent lively debate. It is meant as an introduction for readers who are not themselves professional researchers but who want to know what the discussion is all about – students, teachers and others generally interested in the subject. The authors, rather than either taking a strongly partisan line or suppressing their own critical faculties, set out the arguments and the problems as fairly as they can, and attempt a critical summary and explanation of them from their own judgement. The discipline now embraces so wide a field in the study of the human past that it would be inappropriate for each book to follow an identical plan, but all volumes will normally contain an extensive descriptive bibliography.

The series is not meant to provide all the answers but to help readers to see the problems clearly enough to form their own conclusions. We shall never agree in history, but the discipline will be well served if we know what we are disagreeing about, and why.

T. C. SMOUT

University of Edinburgh   *Editor*

Contents

Acknowledgements

I wish to thank Professors Derek Aldcroft, Heywood Fleisig, David Katzman and Peter Temin for their extremely helpful comments on an earlier draft of this paper.

Note on References

References in the text within square brackets relate to the entries in the Select Bibliography.

1 Introduction

THE slump which began in 1929 and soon enveloped every manufacturing nation as well as primary producing countries all over the world was regarded by contemporaries as no ordinary depression. Although not the longest period of unremitting gloom in recent world history, it was, by almost any indicator, the most severe. Rising unemployment, falling money incomes, the rapid growth of underutilised capacity, the drop in primary-product prices and the collapse of international trade combined to depress the international economy in a way few, if any, serious economic thinkers had thought possible. In 1931 J. M. Keynes said in the course of a public lecture,

> We are today in the middle of the greatest economic catastrophe – the greatest catastrophe due almost entirely to economic causes – of the modern world . . . the view is held in Moscow that this is the last, the culminating crisis of capitalism and that our existing order of society will not survive it . . . there is a possibility that when this crisis is looked back upon by the economic historian of the future it will be seen to mark one of the major turning points [Keynes, 1931].

There were few in the audience, or among those who read the published lecture later, who would have dismissed Keynes's statement as overdramatisation.

In fact, as the depression worsened, some economists suggested that a fundamental change had taken place in the economy of the United States and in other economies in the world also. The depression, they claimed, marked a watershed in economic history because it was not merely a cyclical downturn but the start of secular stagnation. The most prominent member of the school, Alvin Hansen, claimed that the growth which the

9

American economy had experienced in the late nineteenth century had been owing to forces such as rapid population growth, the opening up of new territories and technological growth. By the 1930s, technological growth, itself now weaker, could not make up for the deficiencies in the other variables and the result was a shortage of private investment opportunities, the inevitable product of economic maturity [Hansen]. Whether the downturn was cyclical or secular in character it made an impact which the nineteenth-century depressions, or even that of 1920–1, failed to achieve. The worsening economic situation imposed such a strain that existing institutions were unable to cope; in the most severely affected countries they crumbled, giving way to the varied economic policies of the 1930s, of which the New Deal, the National Socialist economy and the widespread acceptance of economic nationalism are but a few examples.

Paramount in the minds of most people was the spectre of unemployment. Unfortunately, the statistics, even for those countries which had unemployment insurance schemes, have deficiencies. Moreover, it is almost impossible to calculate the extent of rural unemployment and underemployment in the less-developed regions, which, of course, comprised the vast bulk of the world's population. The League of Nations' World Index of Unemployment, with its base of 100 in 1929, rose to a peak of 291 in 1932 before falling to 277 in 1933 and 255 in the following year [LN, *Statistical Yearbook*, 1937–8]. Individual countries such as Germany and the United States were particularly severely hit, but others, most notably Austria, Australia, Canada and the Netherlands, were not far behind.

World industrial production rose steadily from the mid 1920s, only to fall from its base of 100 in 1929 to a low of 69 in 1932 [LN, *World Production and Prices*, 1936–7]. In some countries, however, the peak of industrial production was reached before or, in the case of Chile, after 1929, and, as Table I shows, many countries, including Canada, Germany, Poland and the United States, experienced a far sharper contraction than average during the slump. Britain and Sweden could claim that the shorter slump of 1920–1 had affected industrial production more severely, but for the remainder the depression after 1929 was unique in its severity, and as late as 1935 recovery to the 1920s peak had been accomplished by only a minority of states.

10

Table I

Indices of Industrial Production (1929 = 100)

	1927	1928	1929	1930	1931	1932	1933	1934	1935
Austria	90	99	100	81	69	60	62	68	77
Belgium	93	99	100	89	81	69	71	72	83
Canada	83	93	100	85	72	58	60	74	81
Chile	74	81	100	101	78	87	96	105	120
France	79	91	100	100	89	69	77	71	67
Germany	102	99	100	86	68	53	61	80	94
Hungary	96	98	100	94	87	77	84	98	111
Italy	–	92	100	92	78	67	74	81	92
Japan	83	90	100	95	92	98	113	129	142
Norway	81	90	100	101	78	93	94	98	108
Netherlands	86	98	100	91	79	62	69	70	66
Poland	87	100	100	82	70	54	56	63	66
Sweden	84	89	100	99	95	90	96	116	127
UK	96	94	100	92	84	84	88	99	106
USA	89	93	100	81	68	54	64	66	76
USSR	64	80	100	131	161	183	198	238	293

SOURCE: *Statistical Yearbook of The League of Nations 1935/7* (Geneva 1937)

After a period of relative stability, prices, especially those of primary products, began to sag in the later 1920s and dropped precipitously thereafter. Once the depression began, the manufacturing countries demanded fewer raw materials, and hence those producing them were forced to reduce their purchase of manufactured goods. As it proved much less easy to reduce the output of primary products than that of manufactured goods, surpluses mounted, prices fell further, the deflationary spiral gathered momentum and the world suffered from what Salter graphically described as the 'poverty of abundance'.

To make matters worse, a series of distressing bank failures occurred in the United States, while in 1931 a financial crisis swept through Europe, culminating in the devaluation of sterling and the destruction of the gold standard, which had been restored in the 1920s. By 1932 the world economy had experienced three closely related economic depressions, in industry, agriculture and finance. Moreover, economic nationalism was becoming the common response to a crisis which appeared to have no other solution, and, as a result, a number of distinct

11

financial and trading groups emerged, among them the sterling area and the gold-bloc countries.

Depressions have occurred regularly since the onset of industrialisation, so the key issue is not merely why there was a downturn in 1929 but why this depression was so severe and lasted so long. Among the more important questions to which we should address ourselves initially are the following. Did the First World War have any lasting economic effect? Did the depression start in the United States or are wider economic forces to blame? If the United States was the source of the depression, what were the most significant forces operating in that country and how did they influence the rest of the world? Economic expansion had tailed off in some European countries before the downturn in the American economy occurred, so it is necessary to know if the origins of the European depression are the same as those across the Atlantic.

Once the depression got under way, patches of light were occasionally seen amidst the gloom and the reason why these signs of recovery were cut short deserves study. Did government policies, for example, make things worse rather than better? Why were the violent price falls after 1930, particularly in primary commodities, not checked by collective government action? Why was the financial crisis of 1931 allowed to hit Europe with such devastating . effect? And, finally, was there any conceivable economic policy which would have lessened the impact of the slump?

2 The 1920s: Sources of Instability

THE aim of this chapter is to expose economic weaknesses, operating at the domestic or international level, which can help explain not just why the world was plunged into depression in 1929 but why the slump assumed the characteristics it did. The most convenient starting point for such an investigation is the first major economic shock of the twentieth century, World War I.

(i) THE ECONOMIC IMPACT OF WORLD WAR I

Many studies of the depression have stressed the dislocations brought about by the Great War, which shattered an apparently smoothly working international economic system [Arndt; Ohlin; Condliffe, 1933; Duesenberry, Kindleberger]. There is no doubt that the war had a dramatic effect upon the economies of belligerents and neutrals, not only during the war years, but also throughout the lengthy period of post-war recovery, for it was not until 1925 that Europe reached again the levels of output that had been achieved in 1913.

In 1913, Britain, France and Germany were the source of about 60 per cent of the world's exports of manufactured goods, the vast bulk of which they were unable to supply during the war and immediate post-war years. As a result, frustrated customers developed import-substitute industries or imported from other sources, such as the United States or Japan. When the major economic powers recovered, they found many of their traditional markets lost to rivals or closed to them by tariff barriers [Schedvin]. However, it is clear that western European countries were experiencing a relative decline in their trading positions before 1914, as the United States, in particular, emerged as a powerful force in international trade; the war merely accelerated this trend [Aldcroft]. International trade grew more slowly in the

13

1920s than it had before 1914, reflecting the self-sufficiency of the United States and the USSR, the growth of import substitution, a higher tariff level and the slow growth of Europe's economy, which meant a lower demand for raw materials, which in turn resulted in a lower demand for her exports [Svennilson]. A glance at the declining groups in world trade shows they include all the old staple industries to which Europe was deeply wedded, while the expanding group – vehicles, electrical goods and industrial equipment – attracted strong competition from the United States [Tyszynski; Svennilson]. Lack of dynamism in the export sector made the financing of imports more difficult, a problem solved, temporarily, by capital imports from the United States. The spread of industrialisation encouraged by the war affected Europe's traditional exports, but it also raised incomes in the newly industrialising countries and increased their demand for imports of manufactures [Hilgerdt], though not, of course, the same imports as before. Western Europe's failure to produce the right manufactured exports was one important reason for her poor trade performance in the 1920s.

Within Europe markets changed as the peace-treaty settlements recast the political boundaries of central and eastern Europe, creating a large number of new states. Unfortunately, though not surprisingly, the boundaries were redrawn with scant regard for economic viability, and as a result these new, economically weak states strove to be as self-sufficient as possible, by expanding exports and raising tariff barriers [Condliffe, 1950; Hodson]: at the same time they were obliged to borrow heavily from richer nations. These countries also faced the additional problems of rising populations, which further depressed their already low incomes. The war was therefore responsible for an increase in the barriers to trade and population movement within Europe, which contributed to its economic problems.

Nowhere was Europe more severely hit by the war than in agriculture, a sector which employed more labour than all other industries together. Throughout the conflict cereal output, the main European crop, declined, in spite of desperate attempts to increase it. A shortage of labour, horsepower and fertiliser explains why Europe could not feed itself in 1919 and had to import food, on credit, from the United States [LN 1943]. The withdrawal of Russia, traditionally the granary of the

14

continent, from world trade in 1917 increased Europe's dependence on other continents; countries overseas responded by raising the output of their primary products, financing the expansion by borrowing from the United States. However, by 1925 European agriculture was back to its 1913 levels of production and seemed set to increase output even more. At the same time, production in the rest of the world, encouraged by the golden years of high prices between 1914 and 1920, was at a much higher level than in 1913.

W. A. Lewis [1952] has calculated that, if the trend of output established between 1881 and 1913 in European manufacturing had been maintained, the level of output that Europe eventually reached in 1929 would have been achieved in 1921. If Lewis is correct, the war set back Europe's industrial growth by eight years. It would be a grave mistake to assume, however, that all economic events of the 1920s can be traced back to the war. The economic expansion of France in this decade, for example, is a continuation of a pre-1914 trend; the overseas trade of both Britain and Germany showed a similar structure in the post-war era to that before 1914; and Britain's staple industries would have posed a problem even if there had been no war. A further example of continuity can be found in the pattern of cyclical fluctuations in the inter-war period. In 1914, most major industrial countries were poised on the edge of a recession, which the war delayed until 1920–1. The next major downturn began in 1929 and can be seen as a return to the normal pattern of the trade cycle [Aldcroft and Fearon]. Throughout the world many countries were strengthened by the war, as their economies became more diversified and more committed to manufacturing. In Europe, however, the picture was bleak, for even by the late 1920s agriculture was not prosperous, trade was relatively depressed and in most industrial nations unemployment was high. These problems were not caused by the war but were intensified by it, and, while they offer no explanation as to why the depression began in 1929, we can accept the view that structural problems can lessen resistance to depression and make recovery more difficult.

The greatest cost of the war in terms of instability is to be found in the way international indebtedness was increased, capital flows were changed and the gold-exchange standard adopted.

The war altered the financial balance of the world, and the manner in which the major economies chose to deal with this new situation will be examined in the following sections.

(ii) INTERNATIONAL CAPITAL FLOWS AND INDEBTEDNESS

In the nineteenth century the vigorous American economy had borrowed extensively from Europe, and it remained a net borrower right up to 1914. By 1918 a transformation had taken place, as Britain had been forced not only to liquidate many of her North American investments but also to borrow large sums of money from the United States. France, too, had borrowed from the United States and also from Britain, as well as suffering great losses on her foreign investments in eastern Europe. As the war progressed, many primary producing countries found that they needed to borrow more foreign capital; in the past they had turned to the London capital market, but now the only source was New York. Thus, a combination of overseas lending and the liquidation of foreign-owned stock enabled the United States to emerge from the war as the leading creditor nation of the world, a position previously held by Britain. The cessation of hostilities brought no change, for during the boom of 1919–20 Europe was only able to export goods worth $ 5000 million but had to import goods worth $17,500 million [LN 1943]. This yawning deficit had to be financed by further borrowing, especially from the United States, which financed some 80 per cent of post-war relief credits [LN 1943].

To the war debts and the post-war relief loans we can add a third type of debt, reparations, the sum the Germans were to pay the victors for having started, or, more accurately, for having lost, the war. The total amount of these three categories of inter-government debts was enormous, and involved no fewer than twenty-eight countries: that is, every European belligerent, every new European state, every European neutral except Spain, as well as the United States and Japan. At opposite ends of this spectrum were Germany, with eleven creditors, and the United States, which was owed about 40 per cent of the total receipts from its sixteen debtors [Moulton and Pasvolsky]. The United States pressed for payment of war debts and relief loans, but also held that the issue of reparations was solely the concern of

European states; as a result, there could be no collective reduction of all debts and a unilateral reduction was impossible. There was little support for Keynes's view [1919] that reparations should be decreased; the French, in particular, looked upon them as vital for the finance of reconstruction and for the repayment of their debts.

The slump of 1920–1 brought intergovernmental relief loans to a halt, and the inflations in central Europe deterred private foreign investment, but by 1924 the currency problems of these countries seemed to have been solved and from this date private overseas investment grew in the manner outlined in Table II (p. 18). The figures show that the leading international lender in the 1920s was the United States and the principal recipient of capital was Germany. Britain continued to be an important source of new foreign capital, but, with a weaker balance of payments, she was no longer the dominant power she had been before 1914. Another interesting feature which emerges from this table is the reversal which took place in the movement of French capital, after a peak outward flow in 1927.

During the 1920s, US holdings of foreign securities more than trebled and direct investments doubled as money flowed to Latin America, Canada, France, Belgium, Sweden, Austria and above all, Germany. Britain, on the other hand, contributed little to European issues, concentrating instead upon the Dominions, especially Australia and New Zealand. The money was absorbed by public utilities, distribution processing and financial services, and only a little found its way into the manufacturing sector. Many contemporaries asssumed that the capital flows of the 1920s were identical, in principle, to those which had taken place before 1914, but this parallel was false. For example, one striking feature about capital flows during this decade is that they were not just going from rich countries to those striving to emulate their path to industrialisation, but to nations which were already industrialised and whose per capita incomes were high. Moreover, the US economy, unlike that of Britain, had a low propensity to import; consequently, its debtors had to earn a surplus with other countries in order to repay their US loans. If the ability of debtors to pay through bilateral trade had been the main concern, Britain, which had an import surplus with Europe, should have invested there and not the United States.

Table II

International Capital Movements: Net Inward (+) or Outward (−) Flows, Selected Countries (US$ million)

	1925	1926	1927	1928	1929	1930	1931	1932
Creditor nations								
Great Britain	−261	+126	−385	−569	−574	−112	+313	+179
France	−450	−483	−504	−236	+20	+257	+791	+917
Switzerland	−48	−54	−92	−94	−86	−36	+370	+94
Netherlands	−70	−67	−95	−73	−75	−66	+259	+76
United States								
Long-term capital	−543	−696	−991	−798	−240	−221	+215	+257
Short-term capital	−106	+419	+585	−348	−4	−479	−637	−446
Debtor nations								
Germany								
Long-term capital	+289	+346	+424	+426	+157	+266	+43	+3
Short-term capital	+549	−170	+613	+541	+325	−137	−583	−106
Argentina	+145	+111	+61	+131	−10	+287	−89	+10
Australia	+150	+232	+187	+209	+250	+40	−50	−31

SOURCE: *International Capital Movement in the Interwar Years* (UN 1949)

NOTE: The nature of the statistics make it, in many cases, impossible to distinguish between long-term and short-term capital movements, and even the former should be used only to indicate trends.

Finally, in the years before 1914, Britain was a free-trade nation, and those who borrowed found they could export the goods they had produced, in part payment of the debt. The United States, in sharp contrast, was surrounded by a high tariff wall, though it is likely that her self-sufficiency was a greater barrier to potential imports than trade regulation[Falkus, 1971].

One factor that does require further explanation is the curious pattern of French capital flows during this period. In the years before 1927 the great bulk of French capital exports were temporarily invested on short-term account or in securities bought on foreign exchanges, especially in the United States and Britain, because France was undergoing a period of inflation and the franc was depreciating rapidly. New York and London, therefore, acquired extra funds and this 'hot money' enabled the United States and Britain to lend additional sums abroad, but only while French capital remained. Once the franc had been stabilised by the Poincaré government, the French, now imbued with a new confidence, began to repatriate their 'hot money'. The United States, which had large gold stocks, was able to cope with this capital drain with ease but Britain was not so fortunate. Her gold reserves were limited and, as a result, the Bank of England would ultimately face difficulties converting large amounts of sterling into gold. In other words, during the post-war decade Britain was borrowing short and lending long [RIIA, 1937; Moggridge], a feature which became more and more apparent once the French began to withdraw their money. French funds had given the international lending system an artificial picture of stability, which was quickly reversed in the last few years of the decade.

Yet another potential source of difficulty was the fact that many US loans became increasingly dubious as the decade progressed, and after 1925 the judgement of both investors and underwriters worsened [Mintz]. During the 1920s several US finance houses changed their tactics from the traditional one of waiting for the borrowers to come to New York to the more aggressive approach of sending out agents in search of potential borrowers. This move led to fierce competition, with many agents urging clients to borrow to the hilt [Lewis, C.]. For their part, US bankers found it easy to sell even the most questionable bonds. Mintz's investigation into the eleven leading banking

19

houses, which accounted for about 90 per cent of loans, found that most unsound lending was concentrated in the 1925-9 period, when agents were extensively used. These years saw an increase in US foreign lending to Latin America and also to eastern and central Europe: for example, US investors put up 80 per cent of the money borrowed by German credit institutions, 75 per cent of that borrowed by local governments and 56 per cent of that absorbed by big credit corporations [Costigliola]. Similarly, US investment in Latin America, especially in Peru and Cuba, was also pursued with more enthusiasm than sense [Lary].

Such was the ease of borrowing, especially from the United States, that countries undertook a greater degree of indebtedness than they could, ultimately, manage. When it proved difficult to earn the foreign exchange to pay overseas debt, another loan had to be negotiated to repay the previous one. In many cases the borrowing had little to do with increasing productive capacity or exports, as roads, schools, hospitals and parks were built with borrowed money. It could be argued, however, that capital imports for such projects enabled domestic savings to be used more fruitfully, and it would be wrong to assume that all foreign lending was spent on comparative luxuries or on other enterprises for which there was little economic justification. The early debts incurred by central and eastern European nations, for example, were necessary to stabilise and reconstruct their economies, but even when this was accomplished they were desperately short of capital and needed to borrow. Such was their inherent weakness that overseas investors had to be tempted not only by high interest rates but also by domestic deflation, which demonstrated that sound economic policies were being pursued: as a result, industrial growth could well have been retarded [Bandera]. Imported funds were absorbed by the already large agricultural sector, which in the long run served only to depress agricultural prices further and make payment of the debt more difficult. The capital imports were also used to bolster weak balances of payments, a temporary palliative which did nothing to correct the underlying disequilibrium [Aldcroft]. By the late 1920s, the debt burdens of central and eastern European countries were very serious and for some countries amounted to 25 per cent of the value of current exports [UN, 1949].

20

The crucial issue is to what extent international lending and indebtedness were a source of instability: by the end of the decade many countries had come to rely upon a continuing flow of foreign capital and it was inevitable that any reduction would lead to severe economic difficulties. Several works have stressed the destabilising nature of indebtedness during the 1920s [Arndt; Condliffe, 1932; Hodson] and especially the position of the leading debtor, Germany. All debtors needed foreign currencies acceptable to creditors, so it is not surprising that Germany borrowed, but it is important to note that her net imports of foreign capital were more than twice the amount of her reparations payments. Such borrowing can be defended on the grounds that, if the German economy was to be revitalised, huge injections of overseas capital were necessary: in short, Germany's capacity to pay abroad was determined by her capacity to borrow [Angell]. Alternatively, it can be claimed that reparations were not a burden to Germany since they were paid for out of the savings of foreigners who, in addition, financed an increase in German living standards [Harris; Mantoux]. A more balanced view is that Germany could have paid reparations under normal circumstances, if payment had been a top priority [Aldcroft], but that, in the event of the German economy's entering a depression, repayment was bound to pose a problem.

Debts, therefore, distorted the international economy [Kindleberger] and made it more vulnerable to depression; not only were the amounts borrowed too large, but in addition the economies of the borrowers were highly suspect. Moreover, the use to which some of the foreign capital was put ensured difficulties over repayment, and, finally, a large proportion of the borrowing was short-term capital which was highly volatile [Williams, 1963]: worsening economic circumstances would see its repatriation at the very time it was most needed. A combination of foolishness, ignorance and overconfidence placed the international economy in a precarious position in the late 1920s, from which it tumbled after 1929.

(III) GOLD, STABILITY AND BANKERS

The violent post-war inflations caused nations to look back upon the pre-1914 era with nostalgia, and most decision-makers came to the conclusion that pre-war stability had been guaranteed by the widespread use of the gold standard, which had been abandoned by the major economic powers during, or shortly after, the war. Contemporaries failed to grasp the complexities of the pre-war gold standard, which, scholars now agree, functioned as a result of prevailing harmonious economic conditions [Aldcroft; Bloomfield; Ford; Triffin; Williams, 1963]; indeed, the pre-1914 system of fixed exchange rates and currencies convertible into gold was successful for a number of reasons. One was that it revolved around one dominant financial centre, London, in which the rest of the world had total confidence. Foreigners considered sterling equivalent to gold, therefore London was able to manage the system with relatively low gold reserves; in fact, at this time, Britain's liquid liabilities were far in excess of her total reserves [Lindert]. Although contemporaries had confidence in the stabilising powers of the gold standard, it is worth noting that these powers were untested, for no great crisis had emerged to challenge them. It was, however, convenient, if unwise, to believe that if strains did occur in the post-war era they would be corrected automatically by independent forces [Brown].

The major monetary priorities of the early 1920s were to encourage countries to stabilise their exchange rates and return to the gold standard. Those countries in deepest distress were short of gold and, in addition, it seemed that a decline in supply during the war had led to a shortage of bullion. To overcome these difficulties, the Genoa Economic Conference (1922) proposed an intermediate stage before a return to the full gold standard: this was the gold-exchange standard, which removed gold coins from circulation and put them into the vaults of central banks, and permitted nations to hold a proportion of their reserves in foreign currencies. The practice of holding reserves of foreign currency was not without precedent, for, as Lindert has shown, by 1914 foreign exchange reserves were at least as important, as a proportion of total reserves, as they were in 1925. In this respect the distinction between the pre-1914 gold standard and its successor is not a very meaningful one. The British, however, played a prominent role in establishing the gold-exchange standard, confident that foreign countries would hold a proportion of their reserves in London.

Although adopted widely in Europe, the exchange standard

was doomed from the start, and its earliest weakness arose from the manner in which nations stabilised their currencies. As Table III illustrates, European countries stabilised their exchanges at different times and at vastly different rates, with no attempt at co-ordination, even though all exchange rates and price levels must relate to each other [Einzig]. Those countries which readopted their pre-war exchange rates were at a competitive disadvantage compared with those that devalued their currencies, and they felt that tariff protection was their only safeguard. Particularly striking was the difference between the British and French exchange rates, which ultimately put a lot of pressure on sterling.

Table III

Dates and Levels at which European Currencies were Stabilised During the 1920s

Pre-war gold value of currency restored:
Sweden 1922; Netherlands 1924; Switzerland 1924; U.K. 1925; Denmark 1926; Norway 1928

Stabilisation at between 10% and 25% of pre-war gold value:
Italy 1927 (25%); France 1926 (20%); Belgium 1926 (14%); Czechoslovakia 1923 (14%)

Stabilisation at less than 10% of pre-war gold value:
Yugoslavia 1925 (9%); Greece 1928 (7%); Romania 1927 (3%)

New currency introduced after hyper-inflation:
Austria 1922; Germany 1923–4; Hungary 1924; Poland 1926

SOURCE: *Course and Control of Inflation*, (League of Nations, 1946)

NOTE: Dates refer to *de facto* stabilisation. In a few cases *de jure* stabilisation came later, as in France (1928), Poland (1927) and Romania (1929).

Not just in Europe, but all over the world, currencies were stabilised in a haphazard manner, the sole criterion being an exchange rate that was thought defensible. By 1928, however, most countries had stable currencies and had returned to the gold standard; the main exception was Japan, which was engaged in a major deflation, and finally returned to gold at the inappropriate time of 1930.

23

It was clear by the late 1920s that many exchange rates were in disequilibrium, but having been chosen they had to be defended [Aldcroft]. Overvaluation made balance-of-payment problems more acute, but the countries affected, especially if they were already experiencing unemployment, were reluctant to undertake the degree of deflation which the gold-standard rules required. Similarly, those countries experiencing favourable trade and economic expansion – for example, the United States and France – did not permit the gold-standard mechanism to inflate their economies, so that during the two-year period 1928–9, US wholesale prices fell by 0.4 per cent and those of France by 2.3 per cent [Meltzer]. Even before 1914, central bankers had not always played the gold-standard game by the accepted rules [Bloomfield], but there is evidence that during the 1920s they came to act increasingly as national rather than international financiers [Clarke; Nurkse; Rothbard]; men who were concerned that their domestic economies should not suffer because of gold movements. There was, however, a good deal of successful cooperation between leading central bankers, at least until 1928 [Clarke] – the United States, for example, adopted an artificially low rate of interest to discourage gold inflows from countries struggling to stay on the gold standard, an action which Rothbard 1963 sees as instrumental in encouraging capital exports.

Another weakness in the exchange standard stemmed from its attempt to economise on the use of gold by enabling countries to hold a proportion of their reserves in foreign exchange. This led to a build-up of short-term claims, especially in London and New York, so that a number of currencies became based upon the strength of sterling or the dollar. Loss of gold from one or both of these centres could, therefore, seriously affect several currencies [RIIA, 1935]. New York had ample gold supplies, but London was in a vulnerable position, as reserves fell far short of sterling liabilities. Furthermore, by the late 1920s both Paris and New York competed with London for 'hot money', so that central control, one of the strengths of the pre-1914 gold standard, was dissipated. The fact that there were now three monetary centres instead of one would not have been a problem if central bankers had cast nationalistic feelings aside and acted in the best interests of the international economy. Unfortunately, personal and political rivalries were strong, and it was not clear that, if a major crisis arose, it would be handled in a dispassionate manner [Clarke; Meyer].

As the exchange standard was a temporary measure, several countries began to build up stores of gold in anticipation of a return to the full standard. By 1928 the bulk of the world's gold was in the United States and France, though other countries in Europe, Asia and Latin America increased their holdings also. Gold, therefore, flowed to countries such as France and the United States, which had more than enough to cover their liabilities, or to those whose currencies were not held as reserves under the exchange standard [Aldcroft; Einzig]. Britain, however, saw her gold stock decline slightly, at a time when claims on London which could be withdrawn in gold at short notice were high. Some authors maintain that it was the responsibility of those nations losing gold to check the flow [Rothbard, Robbins], a view with which the French concurred [Clarke], but the more widely held opinion is that the lack of adjustment by the gold receivers placed a great burden on countries, such as Britain, which consistently lost gold [Aldcroft; Clarke; Friedman and Schwartz; Lewis, W. A., 1949]. Gold stocks became progressively maldistributed, which was disturbing, because even though reserves, under the gold-exchange standard, were held partly in foreign currency, it was their convertibility into gold at fixed prices which was the vital factor.

The gold standard broke down during the depression partly because of the way in which it had been restored in the 1920s [Nurkse]. Whereas its predecessor had operated under conditions of equilibrium, the post-war gold standard was restored when economies were in fundamental imbalance [Brown]. Weaknesses in the system – for example, the position of London, and the loss of gold from primary producing countries as agricultural prices fell – became more apparent in the last few years of the decade. The post-war gold standard did not provide stability; it was itself a source of serious instability.

(IV) FOODSTUFFS AND RAW-MATERIAL PRODUCERS

About two-thirds of the world's population in the 1920s had their prosperity determined directly by the prices of primary products, and many countries found themselves dependent upon the export earnings of one or two products. In 1929, for example, the percentage share of the principle commodities in total exports for the following countries was: Argentina, 47 per cent (wheat and maize); Australia, 41 per cent (wool); Brazil, 71 per cent (coffee); Cuba, 75 per cent (sugar); and Egypt, 80 per cent (cotton) [Nurkse]. A decline in the price of any of these commodities would cause balance-of-payment problems, increase debts in real terms and make repayment difficult. The primary producing and the manufacturing nations were linked through international trade, and on the eve of the depression agricultural products accounted for 35 per cent of world trade: the leading importers were the United States and Britain. Unfortunately, the demand for several primary products during the post-war decade, especially from the economically sluggish manufacturing nations of Europe, was relatively low, and as a result imports of manufactured goods were restricted and trade was further depressed [Lewis, W. A., 1949; Maizels; Schedvin; Svennilson].

The size of the primary sector, its pockets of low or declining income and growing indebtedness have caused it to be identified as an important source of instability. The nature of the weakness and its effect upon the downturn of 1929 are, however, a matter of debate. One school of thought emphasises the overproduction of primary produce [Arndt; Condliffe, 1950; Hodson; Ohlin; Timoshenko], but, if we define that state as an increase in production leading to a fall in total revenue, their case is difficult to prove: declining prices are not always an indication of overproduction. For example, the 1920s witnessed an 'agricultural revolution', with improvements in mechanisation and other cost-reducing innovations [Kirk, Kenwood and Lougheed]. Moreover, Fleisig [1972] disputes the view that price falls in the 1920s were serious enough to worsen the terms of trade of primary producers. He shows that during 1925–9 the value of total primary production fell by only 3.2 per cent, a figure which was less than the fall in the price of all manufactured goods. In addition, the value of primary exports rose from $9900 million to $10,200 million, giving those nations additional reserves. Even increasing stocks are not necessarily evidence of overproduction, since such an action could be temporary [Aldcroft], or simply indicate a willingness to hold more inventories during a period of

26

economic expansion [Fleisig, 1972]. It seems that the income of the non-industrial world as a whole was reasonably well maintained, at least until 1929 [Aldcroft; Fleisig, 1972].

While emphasising the global problem we should not forget the fact that the producers of certain commodities did face difficulties: wheat, the most important foodstuff in world trade, faced a reduction in demand, stemming from a decline in the rate of population growth in wheat-importing countries [Lewis, W. A., 1949] and a dietary shift away from grains [Ohlin; Svennilson]; as output increased in the late 1920s, prices fell and stocks grew. Other foodstuffs – for example, sugar and coffee – exhibited similar characteristics. There is, therefore, strong evidence of overproduction in some foodstuffs [Aldcroft; Kindleberger; Fleisig, 1972] and the accumulation of stocks, large when compared with quantities entering international trade, indicates an unstable food market in the late 1920s [Schedvin] There is less evidence of overproduction in raw materials, but, in spite of an economic boom, price weakness and some stockpiling are noticeable in a wide range of commodities – for example, rubber, cotton, wool, raw silk, zinc and lead. Schemes to increase prices were ultimately unsuccessful, because no attempt was made to reduce output; the schemes in fact encouraged producers to stay in business and expand output, thus exacerbating the problem [Kindleberger].

The position that many primary producing countries found themselves in in 1929 was worrying, because they depended for much of their export earnings upon commodities which were declining in price; their problem was that, however cheap their products became, consumption often remained static. The financing of stock holding was increasing an already serious debt burden, at a time when the flow of international capital was diminishing. They were in a state of delicate balance in 1929, dependent upon a continuation of the manufacturing boom and upon a continuing flow of international credit.

3 Economic Expansion 1925–9

ECONOMIC progress was rapid between 1925 and 1929, as illustrated by the League of Nations World Index for Manufacturing Industry, which rose eighteen points during this period; the figures for Europe (excluding the USSR) and North America show rises of nineteen and twelve points respectively [LN *World Production and Prices 1935/6*]. The boom was not a period of uninterrupted national growth, but recessions, such as those experienced by Britain and Germany in 1926 and by the United States in 1927, were shortlived. During this period international trade expanded even faster than production, and the output of raw materials increased substantially.

If Europe's growth is examined closely, however, the boom does not seem as strongly based as might appear. Unemployment, even in economically buoyant nations, was higher than before 1914 and increasing [Landes]; there was also a considerable amount of disguised unemployment in agriculture. Svennilson has emphasised the structural problems facing Europe, with its heavy commitment to declining staple industries and inefficient agriculture, which drained the continent of economic dynamism. Looking more closely, Belgium and France had reason to feel satisfied with their levels of economic growth, especially in relation to their post-war problems, but the other European nations had little reason to rejoice. Elsewhere, Japanese output was restricted by a policy of severe deflation; South Africa and New Zealand performed well, but Australia declined; among Latin American countries raw-material exporters benefited most. The general picture outside North America was of distinct improvement as compared with the first half of the decade, but the prosperity was far from uniform.

In North America, the Canadian economy was engaged upon a period of impressive expansion, but was overshadowed by the

United States, where the last two years of the period witnessed a particularly rapid advance. The principal characteristics of the US boom were: a flow of consumer goods, high company profits, low unemployment, a stable price level, great advances in productivity, a building boom and mounting speculation in property and on the stock exchange. More than 80 per cent of the increase in gross national product during 1919–29 was in the flow of consumer goods, and both producer and consumer durables formed a larger proportion of GNP than in any previous period. At the core of manufacturing expansion was the automobile, the output of which rose from 1.9 million vehicles in 1919 to a peak of 5.6 million in 1929. Other industries much in evidence were petroleum refining, rubber manufacture and radio.

In spite of the prosperity, Duesenberry regards the 1920s as being fundamentally unstable, because the war had led to the simultaneous occurrence of a housing boom, a stock-market boom and a depression in agriculture, all of which imposed an impossible strain on the economy. More specifically, agriculture is often singled out as the most depressed sector of the economy, yet, although grain growers were the victims of low prices, the farm sector, as a whole, experienced a rise in per capita income between 1921 and 1929 more than twice as rapid as that of the non-farm sector [Holt], though the rate of increase was negligible in the last years of the decade [Gordon, 1974]. Only if farm incomes are compared to the very high levels that prevailed during the war can the farmers' plea of poverty be justified.

Structural unemployment was evident in railways, coal-mining, textiles and timber and the US national unemployment figure of 3 per cent has been attacked as a gross underestimate [Bernstein]. In such a prosperous decade it is surprising that 5000 banks disappeared; some were absorbed by amalgamation, but the bulk, situated in the grain states, failed because of low agricultural prices [Friedman and Schwartz; Kennedy]. Perhaps we should not place too much emphasis on these failures, since even the most dynamic and thrusting of economies will have areas of relative weakness. One vital ingredient of prosperity was construction: new activity reached a peak of $12,100 million in 1926, but declined to $10,800 million in 1929. The decline is most evident in residential construction ($5600 million in 1926, $3600 million in 1929) and is held to be significant by Gordon [1951]. However, in 1929 building was still at double the level which had prevailed just after the war, and, looked at in this way, the fall in aggregate construction was slight [Potter; Temin, 1976; Wilson], though the trend was disturbing.

Curiously, for a decade of expansion and growth of gold stocks, stable prices prevailed, though Potter has shown that the choice of different base years and the study of individual commodities reveals a great deal of variation. Between 1927 and 1929 prices actually fell, though not by as much as they declined in other industrial countries, and the money stock failed to rise, a clear sign of deflation [Friedman and Schwartz]. A small group of economists, however, see this era as one of disguised inflation: in other words, prices should have fallen rapidly, but were prevented from doing so by the policies of the Federal Reserve Board, which expanded credit in order to keep the price level stable. They believe that the effects of this action were damaging for several reasons: the increase in bank credit led to a boom in the stock and property markets; the inflation was so distorting that the depression was inevitably a period of violent readjustment; and, finally, if prices had fallen, the standard of living of the whole population could have risen and so, therefore, would have consumption [Palyi; Robbins; Rothbard]. It is doubtful, however, that the Reserve Board was capable of managing the price level so successfully [Wicker], though the issue of income distribution is one to which we shall return. The weight of opinion is with the deflationists, and Aldcroft described the period accurately as one of structural deflation within a cyclical boom.

4   The Depression

UNFORTUNATELY, statistical inadequacies make it impossible to establish with precision the cyclical peaks in all economies. One source shows that Germany peaked in April 1929, Britain in June, and the United States in July, with France remaining immune until March 1930 [Burns and Mitchell]. Using different indicators and widening the geographical field, the Brookings Institution demonstrates that a depression had begun in Australia and the Dutch East Indies in 1927, and that by the end of 1928 Germany, Finland and Brazil had begun to experience economic decline, followed by Poland, Canada and Argentina by mid 1929, the United States, Belgium and Italy in the third quarter of 1929, and Britain and Japan in the first quarter of 1930. The Brookings study shows that several countries were in economic decline before the middle of 1929, and that others were poised upon the brink of depression at that time. This section will begin with an analysis of the most important of those economies, the United States economy, during the slump, and will then consider the reasons for the onset of the great depression in manufacturing and agricultural countries throughout the world.

(I)   THE DEPRESSION IN THE UNITED STATES

In mid 1929 there were no visible signs of strain on the US economy: profits were high, wages were stable, as were other costs of production, savings were ample and there was excess capacity in industry. Yet the peak of automobile production had been reached in March, with a figure of 622,000; by September it was 416,000 [Kindleberger]; inventories rose in 1929, a clear indication of growing consumer resistance. It is not possible to ascertain why consumers began to curtail their purchasing in

31

1929 – indeed, one recent work boldly states that the factors which started the recession cannot be disentangled [Temin, 1976]. All we can hope to do is to offer a number of tentative explanations. It is possible that the expansion in durable goods during 1928 and early 1929 was too fast to be maintained [Gordon, 1951] or the very high rates of investment achieved during the 1920s had led to an exhaustion of investment opportunities, which, in turn, led to a fall in the expectation of profit on future investment [Chandler, 1970; Gordon, 1951; Lewis W. A., 1949; Wilson]. The consumer durables of the 1920s were luxury goods, not necessities, and they were often bought on credit: consumers, therefore, had to be persuaded to buy additional goods or replace existing items, and go into debt to do so [Lee, M. W.; Potter; Wilson]. It may be that the market for some consumer goods – for example, automobiles – was reaching a state of dynamic saturation [Mercer and Morgan] and therefore consumer resistance was mounting; the housing market, too, was becoming saturated [Lundberg, 1957]. Company profits were high and wages not increasing, which suggests that only a small part of the productivity gains were being passed on to the mass of consumers [Chandler, 1970; Gordon, 1951; Potter; Wilson], and there is some evidence to show that the rate of increase in consumption was slowing down in 1928 and 1929, though not by as much as it had done in 1924–5 [Wilson]. This view has been challenged by Temin [1976], who shows that the ratio of consumption to national income was not falling in the 1920s, and concludes that the underconsumption view is untenable. Others have tried to show that income was becoming progressively maldistributed [Brookings, 1934; Galbraith; Holt], and, as a result, the level of demand was lower than it would have been with a more egalitarian income distribution. This argument is attractive, even though it is not possible to show that income became more significantly maldistributed in 1929 than in earlier years [Potter].

Turning to monetary factors, we see that there was a reduction in the rate of growth of money supply from 1928, which preceded the cyclical downturn. Furthermore, the policy of the Federal Reserve in raising interest rates, in order to curb stock-market speculation, was a failure, not only because speculation continued, indeed increased, but also because the high interest rates had an adverse effect upon the US economy. Noting that the 1924 and 1927 recessions followed upon monetary restraint, Friedman and Schwartz claim that the same thing happened in 1929. Others agree that Federal policy adversely affected business [Chandler, 1971; Temin, 1976; Wicker], but no one is sure by how much.

A sensible compromise would be to accept that a combination of deflationary forces, both monetary and non-monetary, was present in the US economy during 1929, and that all contributed to the downturn, which was domestic in origin. It is worth noting that the recessions of 1924 and 1927 were shortlived, because monetary policy was expansionary [Brunner and Meltzer] and the demand for consumer goods and housing was still buoyant, but after the summer of 1929 there were few compensatory factors to prop up the falling economy. Indeed, late 1929 saw the first financial shock of the depression, the Wall Street crash, to which we now turn.

One of the most widely publicised features of the US boom was speculation, especially on the New York Stock Exchange, where a combination of optimism, cheap credit and plentiful savings drove up stock prices, although Sirkin has calculated that the extent of the speculative orgy has been exaggerated, and that the marked overvaluation of stocks was concentrated in only 20 per cent of the sample which he studied. Stock prices reached their peak in September 1929, before commencing a steady decline, which gathered momentum and terminated in panic. On 24 October, 12 million shares were traded, a figure exceeded on 29 October, when 16 million shares changed hands, during the most disastrous day in the market's history. These were not the first crises to hit Wall Street in the later stages of the boom, but they were the most catastrophic, for the sharp falls in share prices during 1928 and early 1929 had been quickly checked.

Why did the stock market collapse? Simply because, since the cyclical peak in the economy, which had occurred some three months previously, production, prices and incomes had been falling, and therefore the investor's expectation of future earnings had to be revised. Once the selling started, panic set in, which drove the market down to its 1929 low in November, but even then stock prices were as high as they had been in mid 1928; the really devastating falls were to come in the following years.

33

The effects of the crash are difficult to quantify. Most authors agree that it did not cause the slump, and merely reflected trends already in existence, though Kindleberger sees the event as one of greater significance – the start of the depression. A strong body of opinion holds the view that the crash reduced incomes and deprived business of a cheap source of finance, imparted a deep psychological shock and created a suspicion of financial institutions [Chandler, 1970; Galbraith; Friedman and Schwartz; Kindleberger; Schumpeter; Lundberg, 1957; Soule]. In addition, the decline in equity values could have left consumers in a weak position financially, and convinced them that a drive for liquidity was their most sensible course of action [Mishkin]. However, we should remember that only 8 per cent of the population owned stocks, and that their ownership was concentrated amongst the wealthy: therefore, any decline in total consumption from this source, at least before 1931, was small [Green; Temin, 1976]. In addition, an examination of new issues of stock during the 1920s shows that the major proportion was not for capital formation, but to finance holding companies: the stock market in 1929 financed only 6 per cent of gross private investment [Green]. As for the psychological effects of the crash, it is noticeable that, even though consumption was falling, the economy and the stock market itself staged a recovery in early 1930, international lending revived on a moderate scale, monetary pressures were eased all over the world, and business forecasts for the United States were generally optimistic. American businessmen did not feel they were in a major depression until a year after the débâcle of October 1929 [Temin, 1976]. Whatever effect the stock market had was not immediate, but gradual; as share prices fell during 1930–3, the market was a deflationary force in the economy, though hardly the greatest.

There was a large drop in personal consumption (6 per cent) in 1930, and a 20 per cent fall in the purchase of durable goods, which cannot be accounted for by the stock-exchange collapse, though the effects of the Wall Street crash deserve further quantitative study, especially if we are to learn more about its impact upon consumers. A partial explanation can be found in the sharp decline in agricultural incomes, as farm prices fell steeply. More important, consumers and businesses became increasingly concerned about financing the debts which they had

34

built up over previous years, rather than incurring new ones [Lee, M. W.]. Consumer durables, therefore, were not replaced at the same rate as they had been in the late 1920s, and entrepreneurs revised downward their expectation of future profit. Although the Federal Reserve had reduced interest rates and injected some money into the economy after October 1929, the period from August 1929 to October 1930 saw the stock of money decline by 2·6 per cent [Friedman and Schwartz], though the deflationary effects of this were modified by rapid price falls [Temin, 1976]. In addition, however, a budget surplus showed fiscal policy to be clearly deflationary.

Even if the depression had been halted in 1930, it would have been severe by historical standards – but it continued. Between 1929 and 1933 real GNP fell by 30 per cent, gross private domestic investment fell by 90 per cent, industrial production was practically halved, and farm prices fell by 60 per cent. In the same period, money income was reduced by 53 per cent and real income by 36 per cent; the net income of farm operators declined by 70 per cent. With demand reduced, industry responded by cutting production and discharging workers, so that by 1933 25 per cent of the labour force was unemployed. Among the most seriously affected industries were those that had been especially vigorous in the 1920s: the value of new construction dropped by 85 per cent, the output of durable producers' equipment by 75 per cent, and consumer durables by 50 per cent. In addition, there were three waves of bank failures, in 1930, 1931 and early 1933, which resulted in 9000 banks, with deposits totalling $7000 million, closing their doors. The contraction in economic activity was not uniform: there were signs of recovery in early 1930, again in the first half of 1931, and once more during the summer and autumn of 1932, but, by the time Roosevelt took office, in March 1933, these dawns were clearly seen to be false.

Why was the US depression so severe? Given the levels of unemployment, the absence of welfare benefits for those out of work, which would have sustained income, short-time working, the imposition, from 1931, of wage cuts and the impoverished state of the rural community, it is easy to see that demand was low. There was excess capacity in housing, as people were unable to pay their mortgages or rents, and many could not afford, or were unwilling, to go into debt to buy consumer goods. Entrepreneurs were gloomy: falling prices made them apprehensive, there was overcapacity in industry, and widespread losses were made in 1932 and 1933; hence investment fell below the level required for replacement. As the net worth of business firms was reduced, they were reluctant to spend, and also became less creditworthy [Chandler, 1971], while at the same time banks and other financial institutions faced a loss of confidence on the part of investors. Personal savings were negative in 1932 and 1933, and, in addition, deflation had seriously reduced the value of bank assets. Most of the banks that failed during the depression were single units, situated in small rural settlements, which were unable to withstand the agricultural crisis. The contracyclical policies of the Federal Government, though more vigorous than in previous depressions, were insufficient: monetary policy was weak, and, although there was a budget deficit in 1931 and 1932, it was too small to have more than a marginal expansionary impact.

The situation worsened in 1931, because, after the pound had been devalued, the dollar was regarded as the weak link in the international monetary chain, and holders of dollars began to change them into gold. Coincident with the international events there was a mounting domestic bank crisis, which resulted in the failure, between August 1931 and January 1932, of 1860 banks. The combination of these internal and external drains saw the stock of money fall 12 per cent between these two dates, the most rapid contraction of bank credit and money supply ever experienced in the United States [Chandler, 1971; Friedman and Schwartz]. Acute bank difficulties were also evident when the depression intensified during the first few months of 1933.

Thus far the explanation of the US depression has been a Keynesian one: i.e. that the fluctuations in income and prices were the result of fluctuations in autonomous expenditure. Monetarists, however, believe that the severity of the depression was owing to variations in the quantity of money; in other words, they emphasise the supply of money, not the demand for it [Cagan; Friedman and Schwartz]. Two prominent monetarists, Friedman and Schwartz, show that between August 1929 and August 1933 the stock of money fell by one-third, the most severe decline for a century, and they claim that an ordinary recession was transformed into a catastrophe by the ineptitude of the Federal Reserve Board, which failed to increase the quantity of money sufficiently to offset deflationary forces. The monetary school believes that during the depression the Federal Reserve was following a tight-money policy, and that the indication of this is not the level of the rate of interest, which was low, but the fact that open market operations did not provide sufficient reserves for a banking system faced with depositors anxious for liquidity. As a result, banks failed, and the bank failures were the means through which a drastic decline took place in the stock of money: this was the cause of the depression's severity. Friedman and Schwartz feel that this decline was inevitable to late 1930, but there the crisis should and could have been halted, if the Federal Reserve had shown qualities of leadership and initiative.

A monetary policy aimed at checking the decline in the stock of money would have lessened the impact of the depression considerably, and there were precedents for such action. Why, therefore, should the Federal Reserve Board, which had pursued, with seeming success, an expansionary monetary policy during the recessions of 1924 and 1927, have been so timid and indecisive between 1930 and 1933? The explanation favoured by Friedman and Schwartz is that the death, in 1928, of Benjamin Strong, who was governor of the Federal Reserve Bank of New York, deprived the Federal Reserve of a dominant personality who, had he lived, would have been capable of forcing on his colleagues, after 1930, the expansionary monetary views which he had espoused in 1924 and 1927. Without him, however, the Board lacked leadership, vision and even an understanding of a complicated banking system. Wicker, on the other hand, believes that the members of the Federal Reserve Board were much more concerned with international economic matters than they were with domestic policy, and he tries to show that their actions were consistent through the recessions of the 1920s, and during the major slump of 1929–33. According to Wicker, monetary policy was expansionary in 1924 and 1927 by accident rather than than by design, since the energies of the Federal Reserve were used in an attempt to curb a gold inflow from Europe, but the measures taken to achieve this end led to a growth in the money supply. These international considerations were largely absent, or not so pressing, during the 1929–33 depression: therefore, the Federal Reserve failed to use open market operations to expand the money supply. While a case can be made for the Federal Reserve taking account of gold movements during the 1920s, it is difficult to believe that US bankers could have been indifferent to the effects of monetary policy upon domestic economic stability. On this point, at least, the Wicker view is unsatisfactory.

Perhaps the most balanced explanation of the activities of the Federal Reserve has been put forward in two papers, one by Brunner and Meltzer, and one by Meltzer. Like Wicker, they see consistency in Reserve Board policy during all three depressions, but their reasoning differs from his. The problem they seek to solve is why, during the recessions of 1924 and 1927, the gold inflows, the decline in the demand for currency and for bank loans and the falling interest rates were accompanied by an increase in the money supply, and why, between 1929 and 1931, the same conditions coincided with a decline in the stock of money. Both papers show that the governors of the Federal Reserve were fully aware of the severity of the depression, but decided not to authorise open market purchases because they felt that monetary policy was easy; indeed, some members of the Board felt it was too easy. They reached this perverse conclusion because market interest rates were considered to be the key indicator of monetary policy: interest rates in 1930 and 1931 fell to very low levels, much lower than in the earlier recessions, and therefore the Federal Reserve's Open Market Committee saw no need to pursue an expansionary monetary policy.

The most recent critical analysis of the monetary account can be found in Temin [1976], who reaches the conclusion that the monetarist school has no explanation to offer for the worsening of the depression in the United States between the Wall Street crash and the British abandonment of the gold standard in September 1931; he does concede, however, that there is evidence of monetary restriction after this date. The debate between the monetarists and the Keynesians on the causes and development of the depression in the United States is a vigorous and continuing one, as can be seen by the reactions which Temin's thesis has provoked [Gandolfi and Lothian; Mayer]. The monetary policy adopted by the Reserve did worsen the depression, for a vigorous expansion of the monetary supply would have made the slump less severe. This does not mean that monetary factors were the sole cause, or even the most important cause, of the crisis: it does, however, make it essential to consider these factors, in order to obtain a more complete understanding of this period.

(ii) THE DEPRESSION SPREADS

The European country most severely affected by the depression was Germany, whose economy was so weak that it was unable to cope with the drying-up of US capital imports [Aldcroft; Angell; Arndt; Clarke; Falkus, 1975; Landes; Ohlin; Schmidt]. The effect of the higher interest rates adopted by the United States in 1928 was to attract foreign money to the United States, and retain capital which would otherwise have gone overseas. As a result, Germany was forced to borrow in London and Paris; Britain found the additional pressure unwelcome, and, although French short-term funds did flow to Berlin, these were unable to compensate for the decline in US lending. The conventional argument is that without international loans Germany had to cope with a growing scarcity of credit, while at the same time having to discharge debts and correct the gap in the balance of payments, which imported capital had covered. Temin [1971, 1976] has challenged this view, claiming that there was no credit crisis in Germany and no balance-of-payments problem either. He sees the cause of the German downturn as domestic rather than foreign in origin; in particular, he seizes upon the decline in inventory investment as the main cause of the reduction in German income during 1929, which, in turn, led to a fall in the demand for foreign capital. A recent paper by Falkus [1975] has, however, re-emphasised the role of foreign capital, and one by Balderston has criticised Temin's calculations of inventory investment. The traditional case for the onset of depression in Germany is therefore still strong.

The German Chancellor, Bruning, dealt with the deficit in Germany's balance of trade by reducing imports, so successfully that even in 1932, when exports had fallen by 60 per cent in value, a comfortable surplus was achieved. Since Bruning wanted to maintain the external value of the mark and pay reparations, at least for the time being, a vigorous deflationary

39

policy was pursued. Fleisig [1976] maintains that reparations made a more adventurous economic response to the depression impossible, since an expansionary fiscal and monetary policy could have convinced Germany's creditors that war debts were no burden, at a time when Germany wanted to get them reduced. Moreover, Germany, in common with all debtors, was caught in a trap. In the hope of attracting additional foreign capital, she had to pursue deflationary policies in order to obtain the confidence of investors. In addition, since much of the debt was payable in foreign currencies, devaluation had the handicap of increasing the burden of the external debt. Thus, Bruning felt that the only policies which could be pursued were wage cuts and reductions in public expenditure, which added to the growing numbers of unemployed and drove the economy towards the financial crisis of 1931.

Other debtor nations were faced with precisely the same problems as Germany. Raising interest rates, the traditional solution, did not bring in sufficient funds, as investors were becoming increasingly aware of falling primary-product prices, which would make repayment difficult. The fact that Argentina, Australia, Brazil and New Zealand had left the gold standard by 1930 further unnerved potential investors. Other debtors stoically deflated, minimised imports, and saw their scarce gold and foreign exchange reserves reduced.

Foreign capital flowing to Latin America had not only provided resources for domestic development, but had also relieved part of the pressure on the balance of payments, by helping to service existing debts. At the same time that capital imports diminished, however, the prices of most Latin American primary products fell – between 1929 and 1931 the continent's terms of trade deteriorated by 30 per cent. In many countries the conventional deflationary measures were tried, but soon discarded as being a cure worse than the disease. By late 1935, 77 per cent of the outstanding loans to Latin America were in default, as interest payments had been suspended and the repatriation of earnings from direct investments was impeded by exchange controls. With the continent so heavily in debt, and the collapse of export prices so serious, it has been estimated that, in order fully to have met its external obligations between 1934 and 1938, Latin America would have had to reduce its 1925–9 level of imports by 60 per cent [UN, 1953 and 1955]. The decision to default helped to minimise the reduction in imports, so that a catastrophic drop in income was avoided. The cost, inevitably, was a complete loss of foreign investor's confidence.

Further examples of the constriction caused by deflation are not hard to find: Australia, which had, in 1929, one of the largest *per capita* debts in the world, found the shortage of foreign credit, plus a reduction in the price of her principal exports, wool and wheat, forced her to leave the gold standard in early 1930. The government embarked upon a deflation, which increased tariffs and taxes and decreased wages and public expenditure [Schedvin], Another major debtor, Canada, responded to the impending crisis with similar measures, as did the nations of eastern Europe.

A striking feature of the flow of US overseas lending was its revival in the first half of 1930, which seemed to suggest that the depression was over. Why did this flow not continue? One reason is that, as primary-product prices fell, investors knew repayment would pose difficulties, a view which early defaults and devaluations confirmed. As for Germany, a number of circumstances made the investor wary: the growing success of the Nazis and Communists at the polls, the increasing severity of the depression and the possibility of a major dispute over reparations all combined to undermine confidence. The capital flows of the 1920s were private capital and were dependent upon confidence; a nation deep in trouble would find it impossible to obtain loans once this confidence had been shaken.

Apart from the reductions in capital flows, there were two other ways in which the United States dealt further blows to the world economy. The first was the Hawley–Smoot tariff, which was signed by President Hoover in June 1930, in spite of protests from US economists and many foreign nations. As a result of his action, US protection increased considerably, and countries all over the world immediately retaliated. It is difficult to calculate the effects of increased tariffs during the depression, because the widespread decline in incomes and economic activity affected the demand for imports and exports quite independently from tariffs. Furthermore, tariffs may have had some beneficial effects on domestic economies, and these could have offset, to some degree, the tariffs' damaging effects abroad [Kindleberger]. Meltzer, however, assigns an important role to the Hawley–Smoot legislation, claiming that it was responsible for keeping US prices relatively high, thus reducing the demand for US exports, while at the same time imports were effectively curbed. Further evidence is needed to show whether the tariff was a more important cause of changes in exports and imports than was the reduction in the income of the United States and its trading partners. Nevertheless, the passage of the Hawley–Smoot bill, and the international reaction to it, can be seen as an additional contractionary force. The second blow further illustrates the role of the United States in transmitting the depression. As Friedman and Schwartz point out, if the chain of causation of the slump had been from elsewhere to the United States, the relatively faster decline in prices and incomes overseas would have led to a balance-of-payments deficit in the United States, which, in turn, would have resulted in a loss of gold. However, during the first two years of the depression, the United States actually gained gold. If the rules of the gold standard had been obeyed, the stock of money in the United States should have grown, but, instead of pursuing an expansionary policy, which would have benefited the rest of the world, the Federal Reserve allowed the money stock to decline. Thus, the international economy was a victim of US monetary policy, and an especially heavy burden was placed upon those countries with low gold reserves.

If we consider the other creditor nations, we see that France and Sweden maintained a high level of economic activity until well into 1930, though both countries were beginning to experience a fall in exports, which increased as the depression progressed. For Britain, one of the crucial factors was that on the eve of the depression about 40 per cent of her exports were absorbed by primary producing countries, which, once the price of their exports fell, were unable to maintain their purchases of British goods [Corner]; thus, the British depression was not domestic in origin, but imported [Richardson]. As the performance of the British export sector worsened in 1930 and 1931, it led to an increasing trade imbalance; as a result, British overseas lending was restricted – new overseas issues, which had been £143 million in 1928, fell to £96 million in 1929, stabilised at £98 million in 1930, but dropped to £41 million in 1931. The main features of the British depression up to 1931 were a sharp fall in exports, a decline in industrial production, and an increase in unemployment, especially in the old staple industries; nevertheless, consumer expenditure was still growing and there was no great drop in gross domestic investment. The misery was concentrated in those sectors of the economy which had, because of structural problems, been depressed throughout the 1920s.

The elements in the world depression up to late 1930 can be summarised as follows.

(1) The drying-up of capital flows was a particularly severe shock, which led to a decrease in investment and a resultant decline in economic activity in debtor countries.

(2) With long-term lending reduced, and short-term capital loans repatriated, debtors found their balances of payments under a new strain. As a result, the total gold reserves of the eighteen European debtor nations fell, from $1503 million in 1928 to $1059 million in 1931. At the same time, the six creditor nations of Europe found that their total gold reserves had increased, from $1987 million in 1928 to $4214 million in 1931, though the bulk of the gold, $2699 million, was in the possession of France, which, as can be seen from Table II, continued to absorb capital throughout the depression [Nurkse].

(3) As the US boom faltered, the United States reduced her imports, yet the pattern of world trade in the 1920s had depended upon a high level of exports to her. Europe balanced its trade deficit with the United States partly through capital imports, and partly through its surpluses with primary producers, who themselves were dollar earners, or recipients of capital from the United States.

(4) A dominant feature of the deflation, in 1930, was the fall in primary-product prices, which made it impossible for agricultural countries to cope with the decline in capital imports, especially as the decline in manufacturing prices – that is, the prices of the goods which they imported – was not nearly so severe.

(5) Economic shocks were felt most severely by countries heavily in debt.

(6) In most non-debtor nations, the deflation of 1930 was severe but orderly. The main exception was the United States,

which late in 1930 experienced the first of a wave of bank failures. But in every country unemployment was rising and income falling, and, as deflationary policies were being pursued, there was little prospect of recovery in 1931.

5 The Financial Crisis of 1931 and the Demise of the Gold Standard

ALTHOUGH the gold-exchange standard had been adopted to promote and to preserve financial stability, its operation after 1929 showed all its inadequacies. A system of fixed exchange rates, like the gold exchange standard, connects prices and incomes in the different countries which adopt it. Therefore, any major contraction involving a fall in prices in one country must spread to others through the balance of payments. The situation was made potentially more unstable because the countries acquiring gold up to 1931 sterilised it, and, as a result, those losing gold, who often had minimal reserves, found that the full burden of adjustment fell upon their economies. The gold-exchange standard thus made the international financial system more vulnerable to disturbances, not less [Friedman and Schwartz].

In retrospect, it is obvious that the gold standard began to break up in 1928, when capital flows were checked, while at the same time France decided to take nothing but gold in settlement of the huge surplus accruing to her from the repatriation of capital and from the current balance of payments [Nurkse; Williams, 1962]. The gold-exchange standard permitted countries to hold part of their reserves in claims against foreign currencies, usually sterling or the dollar. As a result, by 1929 nearly 20 per cent of official international reserves were in this form; for nations other than the United States, France and Britain the figure was much higher [Chandler, 1971]. The system could work only as long as those nations that held claims in a foreign currency continued to feel that the currency would hold its value in terms of gold. Suspicion that devaluation was a possibility encouraged holders to exchange it for gold, or for a currency which was considered safer.

The financial crisis of 1931 first reared its head in Austria, in May, when it became known that the nation's largest bank, the Credit-Anstalt, was in difficulties. This bank had lent on a long-term basis to firms which had become victims of the depression, but it also had short-term debts to foreigners, totalling $100 million. International loans were mobilised to help Austria but never on the scale needed; instead, reliance was placed upon standstill agreements, in which Austria's foreign creditors agreed not to withdraw their outstanding claims. However, investors came to doubt the ability of Austria's creditors, which included Germany, to meet their obligations, now that some of their assets were frozen [Clarke]. The central bankers had failed to recognise that the Austrian problem was part of an international crisis, and hence that piecemeal aid was inadequate. This is illustrated by the experience of Austria's neighbours, especially Hungary and Poland, to whom the Credit-Anstalt was an important source of short-term capital; once deprived of its resources, their limited gold and foreign-exchange reserves fell, and by July 1931 Hungary had imposed exchange control [Bandera].

As the financial deterioration in Austria gathered pace, investors grew apprehensive about Germany, whose banks had also lent to industry on a long-term basis and were therefore lacking in liquidity [Williams, 1963]. German banks, too, had a huge amount of foreign debt, about 40 per cent of it American, and if this were frozen the US banking system would be seriously affected. In June 1931, therefore, President Hoover proposed a year-long moratorium on intergovernmental debt payments, but his action, which was a belated recognition of the links between reparations and the war-debt payments to the United States by Britain and France, came too late. In July, a run began on a number of German banks and capital continued to leave the country. Further deflation now not only made the depression worse but also led to additional support for extremist political parties and increased the clamour to abandon reparations. Who could help Germany? Britain was in no position to offer substantial long-term credit; the United States not only sterilised its gold, but actually reduced the money stock as well, thus thrusting an even deeper burden on debtor countries [Friedman and Schwartz]. France alone was capable of assisting Germany, but was now so concerned about the possible loss of reparations and the rise of the Nazis that aid was offered conditional upon, among other things, the abandonment of a proposed Austro-German Customs Union and the recommencement of full reparations payments at the end of the Hoover moratorium. These conditions were politically impossible for a German government to accept.

Clarke has pointed out that the co-operation between central bankers, which was successful up to 1928, disintegrated during the depression. Part of the problem was that the bankers had never faced a major crisis before and therefore had no idea how to deal with one. In addition, they lacked unity of purpose: France wanted to use her powerful position for political purposes, and the United States refused to consider an overall reduction in world debts. It is not surprising that in July 1931 Germany adopted exchange control [Landes].

Even before July, sterling had already come under pressure. Britain's net short-term liabilities were double her gold reserves, and during 1931 the holders of short-term capital lost confidence in sterling. They noted a budget deficit, the freezing of some British assets in countries which had adopted exchange control, an adverse balance of payments and the overvaluation of the pound; in addition, there was a feeling that the Labour government could not tackle these problems with sufficient orthodoxy. The government, however, responded to the pressure by raising the bank rate and accepting government and private credits from France and the United States. In addition, a dose of deflation strong enough to cause the break up of the Labour Party was imposed upon the economy. All these measures were in vain, for, although Williams [1963] suggests that an earlier jump in interest rates might have saved sterling, it is more likely that nothing could have done so [Aldcroft; Clarke]; in September, the speculation against the pound was so strong that Britain left the gold standard, the first major nation to do so, and devalued by 30 per cent.

The response of other countries, especially those linked to Britain by trade, was to take a similar course of action. At the end of 1931, the British dominions except South Africa, the three Scandinavian countries, Japan and many others had deserted gold. A small group, which included the United States, France, Belgium, Switzerland and the Netherlands, however, strove to maintain the gold standard. These countries now found themselves at a serious competitive disadvantage with those that had devalued their currencies, so extra efforts had to be made in order to reduce costs; in addition, tariffs, quotas and exchange control were used extensively. Germany, for example, chose not to devalue, even though the Reichsmark came under further pressure: instead, in December 1931, the government introduced a deflationary package of great severity. By early 1932 the Reichsmark was stable, and in the spring the Lausanne Conference all but abolished reparations. National income, however, had been reduced by 60 per cent, most international loans were in default and over one-third of the labour force was unemployed.

The depression succeeded in destroying the intergovernmental debt structure which had been spawned by the First World War. When the Hoover moratorium came to an end in 1932, only small token payments were made, by a few governments, and then came a virtual cessation of all payments. It had not been the intention of the United States to release nations so easily from their debts, but attempts to negotiate repayment were unsuccessful, especially as Britain and France, the leading debtors, could no longer look forward to receipts from reparations. The principle of war-debt payment had aroused great passions in the United States, for little return: Lary has calculated that annual receipts from this source averaged an insignificant 0·27 per cent of US national income between 1919 and 1931 – scant reward for perpetuating a deleterious international debt structure.

Britain's action in 1931 not only broke up the international monetary system but also triggered off a further round of deflation in those countries that chose to maintain the gold value of their currencies. We should note, however, that by 1932 the decline in industrial production was lower than average in agricultural Europe, in Latin America, Africa and Asia. This was not owing to monetary factors: it happened because the less industrialised nations were able to protect their small industrial sectors and encourage their growth through import substitution.

48

6 The Crisis in Primary Products

ONE of the most important factors deepening the depression in 1930–1 was the collapse of raw-material prices [Condliffe, 1932; Timoshenko]. Between 1929 and 1933, the world price of foodstuffs fell by 55 per cent and of raw materials by 60 per cent – a much sharper fall than in manufacturing prices. In addition, capital imports evaporated, and the worsening terms of trade led to restrictions in the import of manufactured goods. Why was the fall in primary products so steep? We can begin to answer this question by making a few general observations, since the price falls varied considerably between commodities, indicating that there is no monocausal explanation. It can be argued that capital imports and commodity-control schemes kept prices artificially high during the late 1920s, so that, when international borrowing was no longer possible, surpluses were dumped on international markets in a panic and rapid price falls ensued. In addition, although farm income declined substantially during the depression, output was maintained. Between 1928 and 1933 the production of foodstuffs was stable and the output of raw materials of agricultural origin, which was constant from 1929 to 1931, fell by only 7 per cent in 1932; the output of non-agricultural raw materials, however, fell by 25 per cent by 1932, as compared with average output during the boom of the 1920s. In contrast, the League of Nations World Index of Industrial Production (excluding the USSR) shows a reduction of thirty-seven points between 1929 and 1932, which gives some indication of the reduction in demand for raw materials.

Almost all primary producers found it impossible to restrict output – the natural response of farmers to low prices was to grow more, not less. Mining operations could be closed down like manufacturing business, but farms could not, and farmers in distress could not easily switch to alternative crops. Attempts to

49

raise prices domestically often encouraged competitors overseas to produce more at a lower price; as a result, export markets were lost. In addition, no one who analyses the movement of farm prices should underestimate the effect of weather – the absence of harvest disaster is yet another reason for abundance. One of the results of the failure to curb output was the further growth of stocks: the World Index of Stocks, compiled by the League of Nations, rose from its base, 1925–9 = 100, to 194 in 1932. During the same period the stocks of individual commodities moved as follows: wheat, 163; sugar, 230; coffee, 284; cotton, 161; rubber, 262; and copper, 206. Put in perspective, total world stocks of wheat in August 1932 represented about 20 per cent of that year's harvest, sugar stocks at the end of 1932 were about 30 per cent of production for that year, copper stocks represented 75 per cent of 1932 production and stocks of coffee could have satisfied current consumption for fifteen months [Condliffe, 1932]. Most authors see the stocks as a deflationary feature, keeping prices low even when demand revived, and also making it impossible for individual countries to undertake viable price support schemes. Fleisig [1972], however, suggests that production restriction would not have improved the position of primary producers. He notes that between 1929 and 1933 the world prices of non-food raw materials fell by 60 per cent, while output fell by 25 per cent; the price of foodstuffs declined less, by 55 per cent, but output did not fall. Perhaps, however, if the output of non-food raw materials had not been restricted, the price fall would have been greater.

The fall in agricultural prices was disastrous for individual farmers, who were heavily in debt. Farm price reductions were not accompanied by a comparable diminution in the costs of agricultural production, and therefore farmers were forced to withdraw savings from their banks, delay repaying debts and also ask for additional credit – demands which often, especially in the United States, led to bank failure. The plight of the primary producers was worsened when European countries with large, high-cost agricultural sectors protected them against cheap imports. The wheat-importing nations of Europe actually increased wheat output by 20 per cent between 1928 and 1934. In addition, the USSR, an importer of wheat in 1928 and 1929, became, owing to excellent harvests, a large-scale exporter in

1930 and 1931. There was no single country which could arrest the price decline of a given commodity and no international scheme which could accomplish this feat either.

As a result of the depression, the total value of world trade fell by 19 per cent in 1930, a more serious fall than in previous depressions [Lee, C. H.]. As exports were a vital generator of income for the agricultural nations, the reduction in their earnings was calamitous. Between 1928-9 and 1932-3, the exports of Chile fell, in value, by 80 per cent, those of Bolivia and Cuba by 70-75 per cent, those of Argentina, Brazil, Canada and India by 60-70 per cent. The least-fortunate economies had the bulk of their exports in staple foodstuffs and other commodities with a low price elasticity of demand, or raw materials with a substantial income elasticity of demand; the exporters of dairy produce, meat, poultry and oil-based products faced lesser problems [Triantis]. In addition, the adverse movement in the terms of trade forced severe readjustment on primary economies. For example, Australia during 1930-1 had to export three times as much as she had during 1924-5 to meet the service charges on her debt, and twice as much to buy the same quantity of imports [Lee, C. H.]. However, by 1932 many primary producers had managed, by import restriction, devaluation and deflation, to engineer a better current balance of trade than in 1929, though at a much lower level.

One thing which does emerge from a study of the slump in primary products is the power of the United States, which sparked off the crisis by reducing international lending and intensified it by decreasing imports. In 1929 the United States injected $7400 million into the world economy by its purchases of goods and services and its investments abroad, but by 1932 this figure had been reduced to $2400 million [Lary]. The US depression had also affected other manufacturing nations, and they too demanded fewer primary products. While this lends credence to the saying 'When America sneezes, the rest of the world catches cold', we can see that the infection is largely one-way. Although the reduction in imports by primary producers was large, absolutely, from $10,000 million in 1929 to $3400 million in 1933, Fleisig [1972] has calculated that the effect of the reduction in US exports to this group amounted to about 2 per cent of the United States GNP. Put another way, in 1930 the

51

decline in exports to primary producers accounted for only about 4.5 per cent of the decrease in United States GNP during that year. Therefore, we can conclude that the decline in US exports is relatively unimportant as an explanation for the worsening depression in the United States.

The other major importer, Britain, behaved differently. As the decline in income was not as great there as in the United States or Germany, British exports fell more than imports between 1929 and 1931. This trend was reversed from 1932 because of devaluation and the adoption of tariffs. However, since many primary producers chose to devalue their currencies along with sterling, and, as the British tariff was low and mainly directed against manufactured goods, primary products still found a ready market in Britain. W. A. Lewis [1949] argues that the low prices of primary products should have increased the real incomes of consumers and, therefore, prevented a depression. His case is, however, disingenuous, because the countries whose real incomes were increasing may not have chosen to purchase additional primary products; moreover, they could take their time before spending their extra income, while those whose incomes were declining had to act swiftly, especially if in debt [Fleisig, 1972; Kindleberger]. The depression did not originate in the primary producing sector: rather, the agricultural countries were a victim of declining industrial incomes, increasing trade restriction and their own latent instability.

7 Government Policy and Recovery

MANY contemporaries welcomed the depression, at first, as an instrument which would sweep away the unsound businesses which had grown up in the preceding period of easy credit, and, therefore, enable economies to grow from a sounder base once recovery began [Robbins]. This extreme position is also taken by Rothbard, who believes that depressions should be permitted to run their natural course, as any governmental action merely postpones the inevitable crisis. Few would accept that thesis, and as the depression worsened there was considerable pressure on governments to take action to alleviate the misery. The only country to increase its output steadily through these years was the USSR; all capitalist nations succumbed, and in this chapter we shall examine, briefly, the economic policies pursued during the depression, and see that they acted as a strong deflationary force.

At the centre of public-policy ideology until the Keynesian revolution was the creed of the balanced budget: the belief that a government should not spend more than it received in revenue and, if possible, should earn a surplus to help pay off any outstanding debt. During a depression, however, tax revenue falls, and, if unemployment benefit schemes are in operation, expenditure on them will increase; faced with this difficulty, governments reduced their expenditure and raised taxes in an attempt to balance the budget. President Hoover, for example, raised taxes in June 1932, in a desperate attempt to eradicate a budget deficit, thus further depressing the economy [Stein]. Any job-creation schemes had to operate within this financial strait-jacket, so that expenditure was strictly limited [Hancock, 1962]. Moreover, orthodox economists claimed that it was impossible for governments to create work, as there was a fixed amount of investment in the economy, and job-creation schemes only robbed another sector of investment that could have been more productive [Garraty; Hancock, 1960; Stewart; Winch]. There was the hope that recovery would come from a reduction in costs, which would lead to an increase in profits, more competitive exports and hence an expansion in production. The element of costs most under attack was wages, which had been reduced sharply during the 1920–1 depression, and were cut again after 1930, especially in Germany and the United States. In fact, many economists believed that most unemployment could be explained by the failure of labour to accept lower wages; in other words, if workers were willing to work at a low-enough wage, their employers could afford to give all of them jobs [Robbins; Stewart]. The unemployed were, therefore, victims of their own reluctance, either individually or, more importantly, collectively, through trades unions, to accept wage cuts: as a result, the demand for and the supply of labour were in disequilibrium. It was not until the late 1930s that Keynesian economics was able to demonstrate that reductions in money wages would lead to a reduction in consumption and ultimately more unemployment. However, during the depression years, the popular view was that wages, which naturally rose during a boom, should fall during the ensuing slump. Nevertheless, the feeling of contemporaries was that, regretfully, wages had become more difficult to cut than they had been in previous depressions [Haberler; Ohlin] and therefore in some countries (for example, Britain) industrial wages were maintained. We know too little about the behaviour of wage rates, historically, to test the validity of this thesis.

Also in the sphere of international trade we can see policies which spread the depression. The United States in 1930 implemented the Hawley–Smoot tariff, which raised US tariffs and led to immediate retaliation by foreign governments; by 1932, quotas, exchange control and bilateral trade agreements adversely affected many export-oriented economies. Even Britain, by this date, had abandoned her traditional free-trade role. According to W. A. Lewis [1949], however, the actions taken to insulate economies from deflationary international forces were desirable: it was not a mistake to raise tariffs after 1930, but it was a failure to maintain the high tariff levels once recovery got under way.

As we have seen, economic policy during the depression concentrated upon cutting costs, curbing imports and minimising expenditure, at a time when policies to stimulate demand were needed. There was, however, great public support in many countries for economy: Roosevelt, for example, attacked, as proof of unsound finance, the budget deficits incurred by the Hoover administration, while in other countries politicians of the right and the left embraced orthodoxy with almost equal enthusiasm [Kindleberger; Skidelsky]. The Keynesian alternative had yet to give the expansionists the intellectual tools they needed to justify budget deficits.

It is easy, with the benefit of hindsight, to be extremely critical of government policy during the depression. We should not, however, underestimate the difficulties involved, for governments in the inter-war years were not like those which have held office since 1945: they had far less influence upon the economy. In the depression era a relatively small proportion of the population worked for the government, and public spending, even in mature economies, was relatively low. Consequently, budgets were so small that, even when a deficit occurred, usually as a result of low tax yields rather than of deliberate policy, its expansionary effects were minuscule. Yet, if we consider, for example, the fall in income experienced by the United States between 1929 and 1930, we can see that public expenditure would have had to increase not marginally, but by about 50 per cent, to make up for so steep a decline. The extra government spending required for arresting the depression and stimulating a complete recovery was clearly not possible, given the views widely held by economists, business and the public.

In spite of policy shortcomings, the third quarter of 1932 marked, in aggregate, the lowest point of the depression, though even in early 1933 there could still be doubts that a sustained recovery was under way. Nevertheless, bankruptcies were down, inventories had virtually disappeared, and, as more durable goods wore out, demand revived. In addition, the worst of the price falls now appeared to be over, so that consumers had little to gain by postponing purchases. Some businesses, too, were faced with a growing need to replace equipment, after several years of zero investment. Amongst the industrial powers, an end to the depression was in sight for countries such as Sweden and Britain, which had left the gold standard in 1931, and where the impact of the depression had been relatively mild. In Japan, the devaluation of the yen, large-scale deficit financing, low interest rates and a vigorous export drive arrested economic decline almost as soon as it had begun [Patrick]. The Japanese case was not typical; in general, manufacturing nations depended upon favourable domestic factors – for example, a resurgence in the demand for consumer goods and housing – to get recovery under way and, more important, to sustain it. Even in Sweden, where exports began to rise before definite signs of economic revival appeared, it was production for the home market which was vital and continued to be so throughout the 1930s [Lundberg, 1957]. In Britain, too, the expansion from 1932 was dependent upon the domestic market, where the demand for housing was exceptionally buoyant; in the 1930s, however, unemployment remained depressingly high, as it had been in the preceding decade. In Germany, recovery could be detected even before Hitler assumed power in January 1933, and Nazi economic policies, specifically designed to reduce unemployment, accelerated the improvement markedly, so that by the late 1930s Germany could claim to be the only non-communist country to have conquered the problem of unemployment.

According to Burns and Mitchell, in the United States the trough of the depression was reached in March 1933, some seven months later than in Britain and Germany. Recovery was sustained until the next recession, in 1937–8, because the banking crisis, which had paralysed the economy in the early months of 1933, was resolved by Roosevelt shortly after he took office. In addition, the dollar was devalued and the early period of the New Deal filled consumers, and even business, with hope. The devaluation of the dollar did, however, seal the fate of those few nations, led by France, which stubbornly retained the gold standard. They had already suffered a serious blow in 1931, when sterling was devalued along with many other currencies, and the fall in the value of the dollar placed them in a hopeless position competitively. Unable or unwilling to impose the sort of controls that the Nazis imposed upon the German economy, and eventually realising that there were limits to deflation, the gold-bloc countries gradually succumbed, though France, in spite of mounting economic problems, did not devalue until 1936.

The primary producing countries found the 1930s a sharp contrast to the pre-depression era. All of them had taken some sort of action to alleviate the depression: usually a combination of devaluation, exchange control, default on debts, import substitution and tariff increases. Once the expansion in the manufacturing nations got under way, there was a noticeable growth in the demand for primary products, especially those of non-agricultural origin. The stocks of primary products stabilised in 1932, and even began to decline a year later. The less-developed countries gained some benefit from the depression, because it encouraged the establishment and development of import-substitute industries, especially in the manufacturing sector, but this was small compensation for the trauma which the slump caused. The combination of default and exchange control made it impossible to attract capital, even if there had been willing lenders; the inadequate recovery of some industrial economies, coupled with the growth of self-sufficiency and tariff barriers, combined to depress exports. It was rearmament and war which finally lifted the primary producers out of the depression.

8   Conclusion

THE origins of the great slump, which began in 1929, are to be found in the United States, which, by reducing its capital exports and imports of goods, placed an impossible strain, directly and indirectly, upon the world economy. The economic and financial structure which had developed during the 1920s was fragile, and many economies were moving into a recession in 1929; therefore, when the US boom broke, the general collapse was inevitable. The weaknesses varied from country to country but they are easy to list: the growth of indebtedness, which was not instrumental in starting the depression but was responsible for worsening it in several countries; the ambivalance over the gold standard; the erratic nature of capital flows and the instability of 'hot money'; the weak position of London; the tendency to overproduction in several primary commodities and the structural problems which plagued some industrial economies. These problems were closely related; once the depression began, a chain reaction set in and there was no international body or individual state which was able to halt it – indeed, there are grounds for supposing that collective action, especially by central bankers, became less effective, as we can see from their failure to arrest the financial crisis in 1931. Moreover, the economic policies of individual governments made things worse, not only for their own economies but for others too.

It is almost impossible to decide which countries were most affected by the depression: first, because data is lacking, and, secondly, because comparisons between different types of economies are difficult. The Brookings Institution [1936], using industrial production as an indicator, picked out Germany, the United States and Poland as the worst stricken countries, followed by Czechoslovakia, the Netherlands and Austria. It is ironic that the United States and Germany should be so linked in depression, given the vast difference between them in economic performance in the 1920s, and it illustrates that the reasons why the slump was so severe in particular countries are not identical. The most fortunate industrial nation during the depression was Japan, but Britain too was one of the least affected, along with the less industrialised Denmark and Romania. Among primary producers, the task of identifying the most depressed nation is even more difficult, as indices of industrial production are not a good indicator and we know little about their incomes or employment. For these nations, the 1930s brought a distinct change in economic policy; the capital flows, which had been so vital during the 1920s, were no more, and without them there was an emphasis on import restriction and manufacturing growth and, in addition, an attempt to control, by international co-operation, stocks of primary commodities.

The depression was not the great economic watershed which the secular-stagnation school had believed: the rapid rates of economic growth after 1945 dispelled that notion. The slump did, however, encourage deeper governmental involvement in economies, but often within the framework of economic iso-lationism, and as a result the 1930s became an era of autarky. The depression left a deep psychological scar on all nations – even those, such as Britain, which were among the most fortunate; the poverty, the insecurity and despair are still remembered in urban and rural communities by those who experienced the mass unemployment [Garraty] or the steep decline in agricultural incomes.

Select Bibliography

Unless otherwise stated the place of publication is London

The following list is highly selective and those wishing to extend it should consult some of the more recently published works — for example, Aldcroft, Kindleberger, and Temin [1976] all of which have good bibliographical guides. In addition there are a number of invaluable volumes of statistics, especially *Historical Statistics of the United States, Colonial Times to 1970* (2 vols., Washington, DC, 1975); Federal Reserve Board, *Banking and Monetary Statistics 1914–1941* (Washington, DC; Reprinted 1976); and B. R. Mitchell, *European Historical Statistics, 1750–1970* (1975) which conveniently bring together all the data in their respective geographical areas. Most of the series compiled by the League of Nations' on population, labour, production, transport, trade and prices for the depression years can be located in the League of Nation, *Statistical Yearbook 1937–38* (Geneva, 1938) and *World Production and Prices 1937–38* (Geneva, 1938).

The following abbreviations have been used in the text:
LN: League of Nations
RIIA: Royal Institute of International Affairs
UN: United Nations

Aldcroft, D. H., *From Versailles to Wall Street: The International Economy, 1919–1929* (1977).
Aldcroft, D. H., and Fearon, P. (eds), *British Economic Fluctuations, 1790–1939* (1972).
Angell, J. W., *The Recovery of Germany* (New Haven, 1929; rev. edn, 1932).
Arndt, H. W., *The Economic Lessons of the Nineteen–Thirties* (1944).
Balderston, T., 'The German Business Cycle in the 1920's: A

Comment', *Economic History Review*, 2nd ser., XXX (1977).

Bandera, V. N., *Foreign Capital as an Instrument of National Economic Policy: A Study Based on the East European Countries Between the World Wars* (The Hague, 1964).

Bernstein, I., *The Lean Years: A History of the American Worker, 1920–33* (Cambridge, Mass., 1960).

Bloomfield, A. I., *Monetary Policy Under the International Gold Standard* (New York: Federal Reserve Bank, 1959).

Brookings Institution, *America's Capacity to Consume* (Washington, DC, 1934).

——, *The Recovery Problem in the United States*, (Washington, DC, 1936).

Brown, W. A., Jr, *The International Gold Standard Reinterpreted, 1914–1936*, 2 vols (New York: National Bureau of Economic Research, 1940; repr. 1970).

Brunner, K., and Meltzer, A. H., 'What Did We Learn From the Monetary Experience of the United States in the Great Depression?', *The Canadian Journal of Economics*, I (1968).

Burns, A. F., and Mitchell, W. C., *Measuring Business Cycles* (New York: National Bureau of Economic Research, 1946).

Cagan, P., *Determinants and Effects of Changes in the Stock of Money, 1875–1960* (New York: National Bureau of Economic Research, 1965).

Chandler, L. V., *America's Greatest Depression, 1929–1941* (New York, 1970).

——, *American Monetary Policy, 1928–1941* (New York, 1971).

Clarke, S. V. O., *Central Bank Cooperation, 1924–31* (New York: Federal Reserve Bank, 1967).

Condliffe, J. B., *World Economic Survey 1931–32* (Geneva: League of Nations, 1932).

——, *World Economic Survey, 1932–3* (Geneva: League of Nations, 1933).

——, *The Commerce of Nations* (1950).

Corner, D. C., 'Exports and the British Trade Cycle: 1929', *Manchester School*, XXIV (1956).

Costigliola, F. C., 'The United States and the Reconstruction of Germany', *Business History Review*, L (1976).

Duesenberry, J. S., *Business Cycles and Economic Growth* (New York, 1958).

Einzig, P., *World Finance since 1914* (1935).

Falkus, M. E., 'United States Economic Policy and the "Dollar Gap" of the 1920's', *Economic History Review*, 2nd ser., XXIV (1971).

——, 'The German Business Cycle in the 1920's', *Economic History Review*, 2nd ser., XXVIII (1975).

Federal Reserve Board, *Banking and Monetary Statistics 1914–1941* (repr. Washington, DC, 1976).

Fleisig, H., 'The United States and the Non-European Periphery During the Early Years of the Great Depression', in H. Van Der Wee (ed.), *The Great Depression Revisited* (The Hague, 1972).

——, 'War-Related Debts and the Great Depression', *American Economic Review, Papers and Proceedings*, LXVI (1976).

Ford, A. G., 'The Truth About Gold', *Lloyds Bank Review*, LXXVII (1965).

Friedman, M., and Schwartz, A. J., *A Monetary History of the United States, 1867–1960* (Princeton, NJ, 1963).

Galbraith, J. K., *The Great Crash, 1929* (1955).

Gandolfi, A., and Lothian, J., 'A Review of *Did Monetary Forces Cause the Great Depression?*', *Journal of Money Credit and Banking*, IX, no. 4 (1977).

Garraty, J. A., *Unemployment in History. Economic Thought and Public Policy* (1978).

Gordon, R. A., 'The Investment Boom of the Twenties', in National Bureau of Economic Research, *Conference on Business Cycles* (New York, 1951).

——, *Economic Instability and Growth: The American Record* (New York, 1974).

Green, G. D., 'The Economic Impact of the Stock Market Boom and Crash of 1929', in Federal Reserve Bank of Boston, *Consumer Spending and Monetary Policy: The Linkages*, Conference Series no. 5 (Boston, Mass., June 1971).

Haberler, G., *The World Economy, Money, and the Great Depression, 1919–1939*, (Washington, DC: American Enterprise Institute for Public Policy Research, 1976).

Hancock, K. J., 'Unemployment and the Economists in the 1920's', *Economica*, XXVII (1960).

——, 'Reduction of Unemployment as a Problem of public Policy, 1920–29', *Economic History Review*, 2nd ser., XV (1962–3).

Hansen, A. H., *Economic Stabilization in an Unbalanced World* (New York, 1932).

Harris, C. R. S., *Germany's Foreign Indebtedness* (1935).

Hilgerdt, F., *Industrialization and Foreign Trade* (Geneva: League of Nations, 1945).

Historical Statistics of the United States, Colonial Times to 1970, 2 vols (Washington, DC, 1975).

Hodson, H. J., *Slump and Recovery, 1929–37* (1938).

Holt, C. F., 'Who Benefited from the Prosperity of the Twenties?', *Explorations in Economic History*, XIV (1977).

Kennedy, S. E., *The Banking Crisis of 1933* (Lexington, Ky, 1973).

Kenwood, A. G., and Lougheed, A. L., *The Growth of the International Economy, 1820–1960* (1971).

Keynes, J. M., *The Economic Consequences of the Peace* (1919).

——, 'An Economic Analysis of Unemployment', in Q. Wright (ed.), *Unemployment as a World Problem*, Lectures on the Harris Foundation (University of Chicago Press, 1931).

Kindleberger, C. P., *The World in Depression, 1929–1939* (1973).

Kirk, J. H., *Agriculture and the Trade Cycle, 1926–1931* (1933).

Landes, D. S., *The Unbound Prometheus: Technological Change and Industrial Development in Western Europe from 1750 to the Present* (Cambridge, 1969).

Lary, H. B., *The United States in the World Economy* (Washington, DC, 1943).

League of Nations, *Course and Control of Inflation* (Geneva, 1946).

——, *Europe's Overseas Needs 1919–20 and How They Were Met* (Geneva, 1943).

——, *Relief Deliveries and Relief Loans, 1919–1923* (Geneva, 1943).

——, *Statistical Yearbook* (Geneva): [a] *1936–7* (1937); [b] *1937–8* (1938).

——, *World Production and Prices* (Geneva): [a] *1935–6* (1936); [b] *1936–7* (1937); [c] *1937–8* (1938).

Lee, C. H., 'The Effects of the Depression on Primary Producing Countries', *Journal of Contemporary History*, IV (1969).

Lee, M. W., *Macro-economics, Fluctuations, Growth and Stability*, 5th edn (Homewood, Ill., 1971).

Lewis, C., *America's Stake in International Investment* (Washington, DC: Brookings Institution, 1938).

Lewis, W. A., *Economic Survey, 1919–1939* (1949).

——, 'World Production Prices and Trade, 1870–1960', *Man-*

chester School, XX (1952).

Lindert, P. H., *Key Currencies and Gold, 1900–1913* Princeton Studies in International Finance, no. 24 (Princeton, NJ, 1969).

Lundberg, E. *Business Cycles and Economic Policy*, trs. J. Potter (1957).

——, *Instability and Economic Growth* (New Haven, 1968).

Maizels, A., *Industrial Growth and World Trade* (Cambridge, 1963).

Mantoux, E., *The Carthaginian Peace* (1946).

Mayer, T., 'Money and the Great Depression: A Critique of Professor Temin's Thesis', *Explorations in Economic History*, XV (1978).

Meltzer, A. H., 'Monetary and Other Explanations of the Start of the Great Depression', *Journal of Monetary Economics*, II (1976).

Mercer, L. J., and Morgan, W. D., 'Alternative Interpretations of Market Saturation: Evaluation for the Automobile Market in the Late Twenties', *Explorations in Economic History*, IX (1972).

Meyer, H. M., *Banker's Diplomacy. Monetary Stabilization in the Twenties* (New York, 1970).

Mintz, I., *Deterioration in the Quality of Foreign Bonds Issued In the United States* (New York: National Bureau of Economic Research, 1951).

Mishkin, F. S., *Illiquidity, the Demand for Consumer Durables and Monetary Policy*, Research Report no. 61 (Boston, Mass.: Federal Reserve Bank of Boston, 1977).

Mitchell, B. R., *European Historical Statistics, 1750–1970* (1975).

Moggridge, D. E., *British Monetary Policy 1924–31: The Norman Conquest of $4.86* (Cambridge, 1972).

Moulton, H. G., and Pasvolsky, L., *War Debts and World Prosperity* (Washington, DC: Brookings Institution, 1932).

Nurkse, R., *International Currency Experience* (Geneva: League of Nations, 1944).

Ohlin, B., *The Course and Phases of the World Economic Depression* (Geneva: League of Nations, 1931).

Palyi, M., *The Twilight of Gold 1914–1936; Myths and Realities* (Chicago, 1972).

Patrick, H. T., 'The Economic Muddle of the 1920's', in J. W., Morley, *Dilemmas of Growth in Prewar Japan* (Princeton, NJ, 1971).

Potter, J., *The American Economy Between the World Wars* (1974).

Richardson, H. W., 'The Economic Significance of the Depression in Britain', *Journal of Contemporary History*, IV (1969).

Robbins, L., *The Great Depression* (1934).

Rothbard, M. N., *America's Great Depression* (Los Angeles, 1963).

Royal Institute of International Affairs, *The Future of Monetary Policy* (1935).

——, *The Problem of International Investment* (1937).

Salter, A., *Recovery* (1933).

Schedvin, C. B., *Australia and the Great Depression: A Study of the Economic Development and Policy in the 1920s and 1930s* (Sydney, 1970).

Schmidt, C. T., *German Business Cycles, 1924–1933* (New York: National Bureau of Economic Research, 1934).

Schumpeter, J. A., *Business Cycles* (New York, 1939).

Sirkin, G., 'The Stock Market of 1929 Revisited: A Note', *Business History Review*, XLIX (1975).

Skidelsky, R., *Politicians and the Slump: The Labour Government of 1929–31* (1967).

Soule, G., *Prosperity Decade. From War to Depression, 1917–1929* (New York, 1947).

Stein, H. *The Fiscal Revolution* (Chicago, 1969).

Stewart M., *Keynes and After* (1967).

Svennilson, I., *Growth and Stagnation in the European Economy* (Geneva, 1954).

Temin, P., 'The Beginning of the Depression in Germany', *Economic History Review*, 2nd ser., XXIV (1971).

——, *Did Monetary Forces Cause the Great Depression?* (New York, 1976).

Timoshenko, V. P., *World Agriculture and the Depression* (Ann Arbor, Mich., 1933).

Triantis, S. G., *Cyclical Changes in Trade Balances of Countries Exporting Primary Products, 1927–33* (Toronto, 1967).

Triffin, R., *Our International Monetary System: Today and Tomorrow* (New York, 1968).

Tyszynski, H., 'World Trade in Manufactured Commodities, 1899–1950', *Manchester School*, vol. XIX (1951).

United Nations, *International Capital Movements during the Inter-war Period*, (New York, 1949).

——, *Study of Trade Between Latin America and Europe* (Geneva, 1953).

United Nations, *Foreign Capital in Latin America* (New York, 1955).

Wicker, E. R., *Federal Reserve Monetary Policy, 1917–33* (New York, 1966).

Williams, D., 'London and the 1931 Financial Crisis', *Economic History Review*, 2nd ser., xv (1962–3).

——, 'The 1931 Financial Crisis', *Yorkshire Bulletin of Economic and Social Research*, vol. xv (1963).

Wilson, T., *Fluctuations in Income with Special Reference to Recent American Experience and Postwar Prospects*, 3rd edn (1948).

Winch D., *Economics and Policy: An Historical Study* (1969).

Index